MADELEINE CONNELLY is a qualified ... promotion in UCG. It is through her ... promotion work she became more invo... ...ive medicine – 'Prevention is better than cure'. Current... ...ne works as a nutritional adviser encouraging people to take control of their own eating habits. Her beliefs are that fresh natural foods and a well balanced varied diet are the foundation stones to better health and well being. With her knowledge of diet and nutrition, her culinary skills and her understanding of health problems, she has put together this practical and easy to follow cook book.

This book is dedicated to you –

the promoter of your
own health and wellbeing

NATURAL COOKING

MADELEINE CONNELLY

Complements food allergy tests,
food intolerance tests and promotes
natural healthier eating

MADELEINE CONNELLY
GALWAY

A special thanks to everyone
who helped and encouraged
me to put this book together.

Published by Madeleine Connelly
© Text Madeleine Connelly 2000
© Images Dunbar Design, 2000
ISBN 0 9539801 0 3
Printed by Clódóirí Lurgan Teo
Book design and production by Dunbar Design

Madeleine Connelly
Abbert
Abbeyknockmoy
Tuam, County Galway

CONTENTS

Introduction	1
Nutrition Notes	2
Healthy Eating Guidelines	6
Handy Hints	7
Children's / Teenager's Nutrition Notes	9
Glossary	12
Breakfasts	13
Soups – Sauces – Dressings	25
Salads – Vegetables	39
Lunches – Dinners	53
Breads – Baking	77
Treats	89

Is maith an t-anlann an t-ocras

INTRODUCTION

Food is one of the great pleasures of life, to be savoured and enjoyed. Understandably what we eat affects not only our physical health but also our mental and spiritual well being. In recent years food specialists world-wide have come to realise that by returning to 'Mother Earth' and increasing our consumption of natural foods (by this I mean avoiding processed foods, additives, colourings, preservatives and flavourings) we are improving our health prospects.

Unfortunately in today's society convenience and processed foods are consumed in excess, these foods produce toxins in our bodies which may cause us illness and disease. People need to return to natural, fresh, organic foods as nature intended and provided for.

In this book I shall attempt to help you on this road, the road to better health through natural cooking. Good health means a better quality of life. A well-balanced diet of protiens, fats, carbohydrates, minerals, vitamins and water are essential nutrients for the body. This book contains basic nutritional information, meal ideas, children's / teenager's nutrition notes, recipes and tips. It gives an everyday approach to normal and therapeutic nutrition.

It promotes healthier eating for everyone, particularly people who suffer from allergies or food intolerances. It guides them through natural recipes to make their food lists/mealtimes tastier and user-friendly. It is also important to listen to your own body and get to know which foods agree with it best. Like any machine our bodies need to be oiled with pure positive reacting foods to function well.

Happy cooking and enjoy your food !!!

NUTRITION NOTES

Food is our most basic need, it is also the foundation to good health. Our body requires many nutrients everyday. Known nutrients include: proteins, carbohydrates, fats, water, vitamins and minerals.

A balanced diet is one that contains food from each of these main groups on a daily basis. The following table illustrates the functions and sources of these food groups.

NUTRIENT	FUNCTIONS	SOURCES
Protein	• Repair and growth of body cells and tissues • Assists in producing hormones and antibodies • Supplies energy	Dairy products, fish, meats Pulses: soya beans, lentils, nuts and peanuts
Carbohydrates	• To provide heat and energy • Functioning of muscles	Grains: breads and cereals Pasta, rice, potatoes, pulses, fruit and vegetables
Fats	• To provide heat and energy • Protects the body • To carry the fat soluble vitamins	Butter, cream, full fat milk, chocolate, biscuits, oily fish, nuts and seeds, olive, sunflower, corn oils
Water	• Transporting substances from one part of the body to another- oxygen, carbon-dioxide, cell nutrients • Temperature regulation	Fluids, potatoes (77%) water fruit and veg.(49%) water bread (40%) water

NUTRIENT	FUNCTIONS	SOURCES
Minerals	• (20 minerals and several trace elements) calcium, iron, sodium, potassium, zinc, iodine and copper etc. A good mixed diet should supply all the minerals / elements in sufficient amounts.	
Calcium	• It helps in the development of strong bones and teeth • It is necessary for the normal clotting of blood • It is necessary for the normal functioning of the muscles including the heart muscles and the nerves.	Milk, cheese, tuna, green vegetables, lentils, soya beans, calcium added soya milk, sesame seeds, almonds
Iron	• It helps build red blood cells that carry oxygen from lungs to all parts of the body.	Meat, eggs, herring, green vegetables, wholegrain cereals, pulses, soya beans, beetroot
Phosphorus	• Vital for bone formation • Helps the chemical breakdown of foods	Fish, poultry and meat
Potassium	• Helps regulate body water balance and heart rhythms	Tomatoes, green vegetables, bananas and potatoes

FAT SOLUBLE VITAMINS

Vitamin A	• Healthy skin, glands moist lining membranes i.e. bronchial tubes • General health of the eyes • Growth of children	Cod, butter, cheese, liver, eggs, herring, milk, cream, carrot, spinach, tomatoes, cabbage, peas, lettuce

Vitamin D	• Together with calcium and phosporous it is essential for the formation of bones and teeth • It assists the absorption and distribution of calcium in the body	Sunlight, egg yolk, oily fish
Vitamin E	• Helps metabolism • Helps to destroy harmful free radicals, thereby decreasing the risk of heart disease	Wheatgerm, soya beans, corn oil, liver, eggs, pulse vegetables, almonds
Vitamin K	• Assists blood clotting	Liver, green vegetables, cauliflower, fish, eggs, milk, wholegrain cereals

WATER SOLUBLE VITAMINS

Vitamin C	• Healthy tissue, skin, gums, bone and teeth • Increases resistance to infection • promotes healing of wounds • Increases iron absorption • Required for body metabolism	Citrus fruits, strawberries, mango, melon, green peppers, broccoli, tomatoes, brussel sprouts, cabbage, lettuce, onions, potatoes

B COMPLEX VITAMINS

Thiamine (B1)	• For release of energy from foods • Helps keep nervous system functioning well	Wheatgerm, pork, bacon, beef, oats, lentils, peas, pasta, milk, eggs
Riboflavine (B2)	• It assists cells in using oxygen • Important for healthy eyes, skin and nervous system	Liver, beef, cheese, eggs, milk, green vegetables

Niacin (Nicotinic Acid)	• For release of energy from foods • Essential for growth and the proper functioning of nerves and skin	Wheatgerm, bread, liver, beef, eggs, cheese, milk, white fish
Pyridoxine (B6)	• Important for protein digestion • To maintain a healthy nervous system, teeth and gums	Fish, meat, liver, cheese, potatoes, pulses, bananas
Folic Acid	• Works with vitamin B12 in the production of red blood cells • Necessary for a healthy nervous system and making genetic material, needed for healthy babies	Dark green vegetables, eggs, liver, nuts, wholemeal bread, wholegrain cereals, potatoes, fruit
Cyanocobalamin (B12)	• Helps to form red blood cells and prevents pernicious anaemia	Meat, liver, eggs, cheese, fish

HEALTHY EATING GUIDELINES

- Choose fresh natural foods.
- Add variety to the diet.
- Drink water. 4 pints / 2 litres per day. It is an essential nutrient.
- Eat to satisfy your hunger. Eat all foods in moderation.
- Chew food well.
- Go easy on meat dishes and include more vegetarian meals.
- Eat four vegetables / salads / three fruits every day. They include more nutrients in their raw state.
- Vitamin C increases iron absorption.
- Vitamin D increases use and absorption of calcium.
- Cut down on salt.
- Avoid eating too much sugar.
- Cut down on saturated fats.
- Alcohol in moderation only.
- Dietary recommendations vary according to a persons age, life style and state of health.
- Only use supplements if diet is insufficient or recommended by your doctor.

HANDY HINTS

- Choose recipes and ingredients from allowed food lists / green lists only. Be creative with your food.
- Use meat / fish bones as stock for good wholesome home-made soups. Freeze stock and soups to have on standby.
- Cook extra pulse beans, let go cold and add to dishes anytime.
- Blanch fresh vegetables in boiling water and freeze to have all year round.
- Freeze home-made stocks or gravies in an ice tray and pop a cube or two into a stir fry for extra added flavour.
- Freeze fresh meat and fish to add variety in your diet.
- If you find difficulty in eating fruit and vegetables – make up fruit and vegetable juices, milk shakes and home-made soups.
- When frying – heat the pan first, then add a small amount of oil and it goes much further. Also steam, poach and bake food.
- Slice breads when fresh and put into packets of two or three slices when freezing.
- Store fresh vegetables in a cool dark place and use up as soon as possible to prevent mineral and vitamin loss.
- Wash all fruits well to remove any wax glazing or preservatives that may be used. Go for organic fruit and vegetables.
- Rotate dairy milk or substitute with soya/rice or goats milk for variety and to prevent food intolerances developing.
- Make out shopping list and plan out weekly menus.
- Candida sufferers should temporarily avoid soya curd, grapes, citric fruits and plain white flour.
- If using natural honey instead of sugar use half the amount as it is sweeter. It also acts as a natural anti-biotic.

- Gluten-free baking powder usually contains potato starch so avoid if potato is not allowed. Bread soda is suitable for all.
- If using salt choose natural sea salt, use sparingly and remove salt cellar from the table.
- If allowed – rice, soya, corn, maize, and potato flours and natural products from these foods are suited to gluten free diets.
- Natural foods can be tasty and inexpensive if bought in season, in bulk and by home freezing.
- When re-introducing foods to the diet, bring back natural herbs and spices ie parsley and watercress. They add variety and more nutrients.
- Rinse rice and lentils prior to use.
- Plain white flour, rice flour and potato flour are very effective for thickening sauces, stews and gravies.
- Store oils in a cold dark place to prevent loss of vitamin E.
- To make healthy choices about foods read labels and nutrition notes.
- Do not leave any cooked food at room temperature for long periods where bacteria can grow quickly.
- Re-heating food should be done quickly and at high heat. Do not reheat a second time.
- Combine a well balanced diet with a stress free lifestyle. Take time out to relax and enjoy life.
- Exercise burns up food, increases your metabolic rate and benefits your whole body.
- Use or reintroduce natural herbal teas (approx. 3 cups per day) for added nutrients and improved body functions. Camomile for sleep, peppermint for digestive problems, nettle and dandelion for detox etc.

CHILDREN'S AND TEENAGER'S NUTRITION

- Children should be encouraged to eat a varied selection of foods in order to appreciate good food and develop a sensible eating pattern.
- Meal times should be relaxed, enjoyable and together as a family.
- Get children involved in the shopping, cooking and preparation of food as they may eat what they prepare themselves.
- Fresh air and exercise help to build up a healthy appetite.
- Children should not be over tired or hungry at meal times or they may lose interest in the food. Meals should be served at regular times each day.
- Serve food attractively in small portions. Remove bones and gristle from meats and fish. Make food as interesting as possible.
- Feed children protein foods for development and growth i.e. meat, fish, eggs and pulses.
- Encourage children to eat fruit and vegetables as they are high in vitamins and minerals.
- Give wholegrain cereals, potatoes and bread to supply energy as children are very active.
- Milky foods, cheese and green vegetables supply calcium for bones and teeth formation.
- Do not force food upon children or use food as a reward or punishment as this can lead to eating disorders and food preferences later in life.

- Use full fat and whole foods to promote growth
- Provide child minders with healthy eating information, particularly if both parents work outside the home. Look at the food the child will be getting.
- Encourage breakfast – the meal most essential to school performance. It should supply about one third of a child's total daily requirements: i.e. cereals, fruit juice and bread.
- Teenagers need a good balanced diet for growth and development. If vegetarian, encourage pulses, cereals, eggs and nuts.
- Liver, meat and green vegetables are good sources of iron, a mineral which is often deficient in teenage girls because of menstruation.
- Consumption of fatty foods, crisps and fizzy drinks should be avoided as they lead to obesity and may aggravate teenage acne.
- Discourage children / teenagers drinking tea, coffee or minerals as they can inhibit iron and nutrient absorption.
- Peer pressure and advertising can encourage teenagers to taste alcohol. It is vital they receive sound advise about the proper use of alcohol and the dangers of its misuse.

FOOD IDEAS FOR CHILDREN AND TEENAGERS

- Home-made fruit juices / milk shakes / yogurt drinks
- Fresh fruits, stewed fruit and fruit salads
- Wholegrain cereals
- Natural yogurt – add nuts and fruit

- Home-made popcorn
- Nuts and seeds
- Occasionally potato cakes / home-made chips / wedges
- Baked potatoes
- Veggie burgers
- Raw vegetables – grated or cut in different shapes
- Omelettes / scrambled eggs / boiled eggs
- Home-made soups
- Nuggets – fish / chicken pieces in home-made batter
- Home-made beef burgers
- Rice puddings
- Rice / pasta dishes
- Nutritious home-made scones / breads / pancakes
- Melted cheese on bread
- Shepherds pie
- Spaghetti bolognese
- Home-made jams / natural peanut butter
- Chicken legs
- Stir fry with rice noodles
- Chicken casserole / stews
- Boiled potatoes and vegetables mashed together
- Fruit crumble
- Home-made ice-cream
- Ice pops – frozen orange juice in ice-cube trays with a pop stick

All recipes serve 2–4 people approx.

GLOSSARY

Blanch	Immerse food in water, bring to the boil and then remove
Sauté	Fry lightly in a little oil
Plain flour	White flour, (no raising agent added)
Seasoned flour	Flour which has salt and pepper added
Sift	Put dry ingredients through a sieve to introduce air
Skinned tomatoes	Cut out the core of the tomato, immerse in boiling water. Remove after 8 to 15 seconds, leave to cool and peel away skin.
Preheat	Heat oven for 10–15 minutes prior to use at specified temperatures
Mins	Minutes
Wet ingredients	Milks, egg, oil, fruit juices, water
Dry ingredients	Flours, brans, flakes, germs, bread soda, baking powder, salt, sugar
Seasoning	Sea salt, black and white pepper, fresh herbs and spices

CONVERSION TABLES

1 tsp = 1 teaspoon (5mls)
1 dsp = 1 dessertspoon (10mls)
1 tbsp = 1 tablespoon (20mls)

25gms = 1oz	25ml = 1fl oz
110gms = 4oz / $^1/_4$lb	150ml = $^1/_4$pt
225gms = 8oz / $^1/_2$lb	275ml = $^1/_2$pt
450gms = 16oz / 1lb	450ml = $^3/_4$pt
1kg = 2.2lbs	570ml = 1pt

BREAKFASTS

Its not the food in your life
its the life in your food

BREAKFAST IDEAS
A good start to a day

- Wholegrain natural cereals (add fruit and nuts)
- Home-made mueslis/porridges – oat / rye / wheat / rice / barley flakes
- Corn maize meal
- Fruit pieces / fruit salad / stewed fruit
- Home-made fruit juices
- Home-made vegetable juices
- Home-made milk shakes / yogurt drinks
- Natural bio yogurt (add fruit and nuts)
- Rice pudding
- Mixed grill (back rashers, chops, liver, fish, mushrooms, tomatoes)
- Eggs boiled, poached or scrambled
- Home-made potato cakes
- Home-made pancakes
- Home-made brown scones / breads

BREAKFASTS

Chopped nuts, seeds, natural bio yogurt and fresh fruit can be added to cereals / muesli to increase nutritional value. As a treat add a little fresh cream, if allowed.

RICE PORRIDGE

225g / 8oz of brown rice flakes
570ml / 1 pt of water

Put flakes and water together in a saucepan. Bring to the boil and cook briskly for a few minutes stirring all the time – serve with milk / soya milk. Substitute rice flakes with oats, rye, millet, barley or wheat flakes for different porridges. Reduce cooking time by soaking flakes overnight.

OATMEAL MUESLI

225g / 8oz oat flakes
1 tbs wheatgerm / soya bran / oat bran / rice bran
Toasted nuts, almonds, coconut, peanuts, sunflower seeds, walnuts
Fresh fruit (grated apple, grapes, bananas)

Toast oat flakes with your choice of bran.
Serve with chopped nuts and fresh fruit. Add milk or water.

TIP
Most nuts are good for lowering cholesterol, they protect against breast and prostate cancer and are good for male fertility.

MIXED FLAKE MUESLI

110g / 4oz rolled oat flakes
110g / 4oz wheat / barley or rye flakes
110g / 4oz cup chopped nuts (almond, brazil, coconut)
1 tbsp seeds (sunflower, sesame)
1–2 tbsp home-made apple / grape juice
milk / soya milk

Toast all flakes in a dry pan for 5 mins approx. Transfer to a dish. Add nuts, seeds, fresh juice / milk.

BANANA AND MAIZE BREAKFAST CEREAL

125ml / ¼ pt milk / soya milk
125ml / ¼ pt boiling water
2 rounded tbsp coarse maize meal
2 bananas very finely sliced

Mix maize meal to a smooth paste with milk/soya milk in a pan. Add the boiling water and banana, bring to the boil – stirring constantly, lower the heat and simmer for 5–10 mins until banana is beginning to disintegrate.

NOTE:
Alternatives to dairy milks for cereals – soya, rice or goats milk
- 2 ripe bananas, 1 egg white, water – whisk or liquidise to required consistency (use from fresh, will not keep).
- Home-made fruit juices / water.
- Soak oat flakes in water overnight, drain and use liquid as oat milk – chill before serving.

TIP
A single carrot will supply your vitamin A needs for an entire day.

FRUIT JUICES

Experiment and create your own

Drinking fresh juices daily is a very healthy habit to get into as they are so easily digested and packed with essential vitamins and minerals. It is best taken 20 minutes prior to food.
Fruit juice protects us from illness by strengthening the immune system. It cleanses the blood and our vital organs and helps to stimulate our metabolism. All these things help to maintain a healthy and vibrant body.

APPLE AND ORANGE JUICE

2 apples

2 oranges

Wash and slice apples and peel oranges. Place all ingredients in juicer. Juice and serve.

APPLE PINEAPPLE AND PEAR JUICE

1 apple

$1/3$ pineapple

2 pears

Wash and slice apple and pears. Peel the pineapple and dice. Place all ingredients in juicer. Juice and serve.

APPLE ORANGE AND STRAWBERRY JUICE

2 apples

1 orange

225g / 8oz strawberries

Wash and slice apples. Peel orange. Wash strawberries. Place all ingredients in juicer. Juice and serve.

ORANGE LEMON AND GRAPEFRUIT JUICE

2 oranges

1 grapefruit

1 lemon

Wash and peel ingredients. Dice. Place in juicer. Juice and serve.

APPLE RASPBERRY AND MANGO JUICE

2 apples

225g / 8oz raspberries

1 mango

Wash raspberries. Wash and slice apples. Peel and remove stones from mango. Place ingredients in juicer. Juice and serve.

TIP

Bananas are high in potassium which is needed for a healthy heart and are full of a useful fibre called pectin. They also prevent cramps and are a high energy food, therefore are an ideal snack for sporty people.

ORANGE PEACH AND MANGO JUICE

2 oranges

2 peaches

1 mango

Wash and remove stones from peaches. Peel and remove stones from mango. Peel the oranges. Place all ingredients in juicer. Juice and serve.

MELON JUICE

1/4 honeydew melon

1/2 water melon

1/2 gala melon

Peel the melons. Remove the seeds. Place in juicer. Juice and serve.

APPLE CARROT AND MELON JUICE

1 apple

2 carrots

1/2 melon

Peel the melon and remove the seeds. Wash the remaining ingredients. Trim the carrots. Place all ingredients in juicer. Juice and serve.

CARROT APPLE GREEN PEPPER AND CELERY JUICE

3 carrots

1 apple

1/2 green pepper

1 stick of celery

Wash all ingredients. Trim the carrots and celery. Slice the apple. Remove the seeds from the pepper.
Place all ingredients in juicer. Juice and serve.

CARROT APPLE AND RED CABBAGE JUICE

4 carrots

1 apple

110g / 4oz red cabbage

Wash all ingredients. Trim the carrots. Slice the apple.
Place all ingredients in juicer. Juice and serve.

CARROT TOMATO AND BEETROOT JUICE

2 carrots

5 tomatoes

225g / 8oz beetroot

Wash all ingredients. Trim the carrots. Slice the tomatoes and beetroot. Place all ingredients in juicer. Juice and serve.

APPLE CARROT CELERY AND LETTUCE JUICE

2 apples

2 carrots

6 lettuce leaves

1 stick of celery

Wash all ingredients. Trim the celery and carrots. Slice the apples.
Place all ingredients into juicer. Juice and serve.

TIP

Cauliflower supplies selenium – necessary for strong bones, healthy hair and firm skin.

CARROT RADISH AND SPINACH JUICE

4 carrots
6 radishes
A handful of spinach

Wash all ingredients. Trim the carrots and radishes, add spinach. Place all ingredients in juicer. Juice and serve.

MILK SHAKES

275ml / $^1/_2$pt milk / soya milk
275ml / $^1/_2$pt home-made fruit juice (strawberry, banana, peach, pear)
3 ice-cubes

Blend all ingredients until frothy. Chill and serve.

OPTIONAL – Add a little sugar, home-made ice-cream, fresh cream.

YOGURT DRINKS

275ml / $^1/_2$pt of natural bio-yogurt
275ml / $^1/_2$pt of home-made fruit juices

Blend together, chill and serve.

GRAPEFRUIT

Cut in halves, remove the pips and core with a sharp knife.
Cut around the grapefruit between the rind and the fruit and cut into segments.

OPTIONAL – Sprinkle with brown sugar and heat under a warm grill for one minute.

FRIED BREAD

Cut bread into slices and remove the crusts.
Fry quickly until golden brown on both sides.
Drain and serve with rashers, tomatoes or scrambled egg.
To make French toast dip bread in egg and milk mixture before frying.

BARLEY WATER

50g / 2oz pearl barley
570ml / 1pt cold water
Sugar to taste
Rind and juice of half a lemon / orange

Put barley and water into a saucepan. Add rind of lemon / orange. Bring to the boil and then simmer for 1 hr. Add sugar and lemon / orange juice. Serve hot or cold.

Particularly good for people with cystitis or kidney problems.

TIP
Sunflower seeds are packed with wonderful nutrients, vitamins, minerals and unsaturated fats and protein.

TIP

Good foods for healthy skin are cauliflower, broccoli, carrots, cabbage, spinach, red and yellow peppers. They contain beta-carotene which converts to vitamin A.

Men should eat the following zinc rich foods for a healthy prostate gland – liver, garlic, brazil nuts, pumpkin seeds, eggs, oats, crab, chicken and almonds.

Sesame seeds contain high calcium levels. They are also a good source of protein and B vitamins. They can be added to salads, bread and stir fries.

SOUPS
SAUCES
DRESSINGS

HERBS AND SPICES

Fresh herbs are full of beneficial minerals and vitamins. Dried herbs are useful as a standby but lack vitamins. They are stronger tasting so only use half the amount. Here are some combinations to try out.

- BASIL – tomato dishes, salads
- BAY LEAVES – sauces, stews and soups
- CHIVES – salads, dressings, potatoes
- DILL – sparingly in salads, dressings and sauces
- MINT – peas, beans and potatoes, a garnish for salads and cold drinks
- OREGANO – tomato, eggs, beans and pork dishes
- PARSLEY – goes with everything
- SAGE – lentils, pulses, cheese and tomato dishes
- THYME – egg dishes, stews, casseroles, use sparingly
- DRIED MIXED HERBS – all savoury dishes
- CAYENNNE PEPPER – barbecues, tomato, cheese dishes, egg dishes
- CHILLI POWDER – sauces, dressings, casseroles and con-carne
- CURRY POWDER – curries, stir fries, soups
- GINGER – stir fries, curries, salads and casseroles
- PEPPER CORNS – all savoury dishes
- SEA SALT – use sparingly in all dishes

Cooking with herbs is a way of developing your own personal style in recipes, so experiment with various combinations.

SOUPS

Soups can be very tasty, filling and a meal in themselves. The foundation of a flavoursome soup is a home-made stock. This can be made by boiling up meat / fish bones, vegetables, seasoning and water. Then simmer for 1½–2 hrs. This stock also freezes very well. The more ingredients added to soups, the more nutritous they are. A little milk can be added just before serving to give a creamier texture.

MIXED VEGETABLE SOUP

225g / 8oz vegetables (carrot, potato, parsnip, onion and garlic)
570ml / 1pt home-made stock
A little butter / oil
2 tsp plain flour / rice flour / potato flour
Seasoning

Dice all vegetables. Sauté in melted butter / oil. Add seasoning and stock. Stir well. Bring to the boil.
Simmer until vegetables are soft 30–40 mins.
Mix the flour with a little water and add to thicken the soup.
Bring to the boil, stirring continuously for a few minutes.
Liquidise.
For a chunky soup do not blend.

TOMATO SOUP

225g / 8oz tomatoes skinned and chopped finely
110g / 4oz carrot
110g / 4oz onion
1 stick celery
2 tsp plain flour / rice flour / potato flour
A little oil / butter
570ml / 1 pt stock / water
1 tsp sugar
Seasoning

Dice vegetables, sauté in butter / oil. Add the chopped tomatoes, sugar and flour. Mix well and cook for a few minutes. Add seasoning and stock / water. Bring to the boil, simmer for 30–40 mins. Liquidise.
Stir well.

TIP
A whole fresh orange at the start of a meal will increase your intake of iron, calcium and other useful minerals.

POTATO SOUP

225g / 8oz potatoes
1 onion
1 clove garlic crushed
2 sticks celery
A little butter / oil
570ml / 1pt stock
275ml / 1/2 pt water
Seasoning

Dice vegetables, sauté in melted butter / oil, add seasoning and stock. Bring to the boil and simmer for 30–40 mins. Add water . Stir well. Liquidise.

MUSHROOM SOUP

Make as potato soup, add 175g / 6oz chopped mushrooms and only 50g / 2oz of potatoes.

LENTIL SOUP

Make as tomato soup. Add 110g / 4oz red lentils when adding stock and seasoning.

CARROT AND ORANGE SOUP

Make as tomato soup. Use 225g / 8oz carrots and 110g / 4oz tomato. Add juice and rind of 2 whole oranges when adding seasoning and stock .

MINESTRONE SOUP

Make as tomato soup. Add any vegetable of choice. Add 110g / 4oz pasta – spaghetti pieces 15 mins before end of cooking time. Do not liquidise.

CHICKEN AND SWEETCORN SOUP

Make as mixed vegetable soup. Sauté 110g / 4oz thin strips of cooked chicken, then add 110g / 4oz baby corns, chopped into small pieces, with other vegetables. Do not liquidise.

SEAFOOD CHOWDER

Make as mixed vegetable soup. Sauté 110g / 4oz mixed fish pieces and 4 chopped rashers before vegetables. Do not liquidise.

TIP

Porridge supplies iron, zinc and calcium as well as the important B complex vitamins. It also helps to lower cholesterol levels.

SAUCES

Add sauces to meat / fish dishes, stir fries, pasta dishes casseroles or baked potatoes.

APPLE SAUCE

Serve with pork / puddings e.g. rice, porridge etc. 2 diced apples, $1/4$ tsp sugar and 3 tbs water. Simmer until soft. Blend.

PEACH SAUCE

Serve with white meat.
Poach 3 peaches, remove skin and seed. Blend.

ORANGE SAUCE

2 oranges segmented and deseeded, $1/4$ tsp sugar and 1 tbs water, simmer until soft. Blend.

TOMATO SAUCE

| 6 tomatoes |
| 1 onion chopped |
| 1 clove garlic |
| seasoning |

Sauté onion and garlic in a little oil until soft. Add seasoning. Add chopped tomatoes and blend. Add a little water if too dry.

MIXED VEGETABLE SAUCE

225g / 8oz vegetables of choice
150ml / ¼pt water
seasoning

Chop vegetables, add seasoning and water. Simmer until soft and blend.

WHITE SAUCE

570ml / 1pt milk / soya milk
75g / 3oz butter
75g / 3oz plain flour / rice flour / potato flour
Seasoning
Little onion / garlic – optional

Melt butter, sauté onions and garlic, add seasoning and flour. Mix well, add milk. Stir briskly over a moderate heat until smooth.

CHEESE SAUCE

Add 50g / 2oz cheese to white sauce.

MUSHROOM SAUCE

Add 50g / 2oz cooked mushrooms to white sauce.

EGG SAUCE

Add 1 chopped hard boiled egg to white sauce.

CURRY SAUCE WITH LENTILS AND YOGURT

1 dsp oil
1 large onion chopped
2 cloves of garlic
1 tbsp curry powder
50g / 2oz red lentils
450ml / ¾pt vegetable stock
150ml / ¼pt of pure natural yogurt
2 tsp plain flour / rice flour / potato flour

Heat oil in a pot. Add onion, garlic and sauté for 5 mins. Add curry powder and stir for 2 mins. Add the lentils and stock. Bring to the boil, reduce heat and simmer for 30 mins. Thicken with flour and a little water mixed together. Stir in yogurt before serving.

SAUCE HOLLANDAISE

1 tbsp lemon juice
1 tbsp cold water
2 egg yolks
110g / 4oz butter

Mix lemon juice and water together in a bowl. Set over a pan of hot water (not boiling). Beat in egg yolks, then whisk in a quarter of the butter, whisking until the butter has melted. Gradually add the rest of the butter, beat well. Do not reheat.
Serve with fish – salmon / haddock.

REAL GRAVY

275ml / ½pt meat juices (roast, chicken etc.)/ home-made stock or both mixed
2 tsp plain flour / rice flour / potato flour
50g / 2oz finely chopped onion / 1 garlic clove (optional)

Pour meat juices into a saucepan, skim any fat from the surface. Add onion and garlic, cook over a low heat.
Mix flour with a little cold water and add to the mixture stirring continuously until it thickens. Serve with roast.
OPTIONAL: Add grated rind of an orange or lemon.

TIP
Turnips are a good food for people with gout as they get rid of uric acid (a build up of toxins in the body).

NUT SPREADS

225g / 8oz nuts (almonds / peanuts / sesame seeds)
2 tbsp oil allowed

Blend nuts and oil to form a paste. Use on bread.
OPTIONAL: Thin down with lemon juice / add garlic and use as a salad dressing / sauce.

TIP
Beetroot contains iron and is a good source of folic acid.

SATAY SAUCE

75g / 3oz unsalted peanuts
1/2 red chilli
2 cloves garlic
1 small onion chopped
1 dsp oil
2 tbsp water

Skin nuts (by heating in the oven or a dry pan over heat for 2–3 mins). Rub through hands to remove skins.
Place nuts in a blender, add chilli, garlic, onion and oil.
Grind to a paste, adding enough water to make a workable paste.
Place mix in a pot and stir over a low heat for 3 mins.
Stir in remaining water and simmer for 5 mins – remove and add lemon juice.
Serve with chicken or as a hot salad dressing.

GARLIC BUTTER

25g / 1oz pure butter
2 cloves garlic crushed
1/2 tsp lemon juice
Seasoning

Cream the butter, stir in the garlic, lemon juice and seasoning.
A little olive oil can also be added to butter. Put in the fridge to set.
Serve with steak, fish or baked potatoes.

TIP

Drink natural fruit and vegetable juices, natural herbal teas, lots of water and only moderate quantities of tea, coffee and alcohol.

DHAL SAUCE

110g / 4oz lentils
570ml / 1pt water
1 onion
1 tbsp oil
2 tsp natural curry powder
Juice and rind of 1 lemon
Seasoning

Soak lentils overnight – cook till tender in water, sauté onion with the curry powder until soft. Add lentils, juice, grated rind and seasoning. Liquidise.

SOYA MAYONNAISE

1 tbsp soya flour
2 tbsp lemon juice
4 tbsp oil (2 olive oil, 2 soya oil)
Seasoning
Grated rind of 1/2 lemon / orange (optional)
Garlic (optional)

Mix soya flour to a paste with lemon juice, gradually add oils little by little and beat until thick.
Add seasoning.
Add garlic / lemon / orange (optional).

TIP
A diet rich in fruit and vegetables helps to lower heart disease and prevent cancers.

SALAD DRESSING

BASIC SALAD DRESSING

120ml / 6 tbs of oil (olive, walnut, sesame seed etc.)
40ml / 2 tbs of lemon juice / grapefruit juice
Seasoning

Mix together and chill.

VARIATIONS:
- Chopped scallions / onion
- Chopped garlic
- Chopped red / green / yellow peppers very fine
- Chopped chilli peppers
- Chopped celery very fine
- Juice and rind of orange
- 1 tsp sugar
- 2 tbsp fresh cream
- 2 tbsp tomatoes pureed

Serve with salads or baked potatoes.

MAYONNAISE

2 egg yolks
2 tbsp of water
1 tbsp lemon juice
4 tbsp of oil
Seasoning

Blend all ingredients except oil together. Slowly drop by drop add oil till it thickens (if it separates add a little boiling water and blend).

VARIATIONS:
- Crushed garlic
- Chopped scallions
- Chopped cucumber

MARIE ROSE SAUCE

Add 2 tbsp pureed tomatoes to mayonnaise – serve with fresh prawns – prawn cocktail.

YOGURT DRESSING

| 2 tbs plain natural bio yogurt |
| 1 tsp lemon juice |
| Seasoning |

VARIATIONS:
- Chopped garlic
- Chopped cucumber, tomatoes, scallions
- Chopped peppers
- Chopped walnuts
- Chopped hard boiled eggs
- Chopped celery

TIP
Brown Rice provides B vitamins, fibre, iron, potassium and protein.

TIP

Pineapple contains vitamin C and fibre and has the ability to break down blood clots. This makes it an excellent heart protector and also treats bruised skin.

Foods rich in iron, folic acid and vitamin B_{12} will increase the red cells ability to carry oxygen. This is very important for sports people as it will increase their exercise levels.

SALADS
VEGETABLES

TIP
Eat lots of raw vegetables and salads as they contain oxygen, hormones and enzymes. These wonderful chemicals energise the body and enhancce the immune system.

TIP
Kiwis contain lots of vitamin C, potassium and fibre

SALADS

CURRIED VEGETABLE SALAD

225g / 8oz broccoli
225g / 8oz cauliflower
225g / 8oz carrots
110g / 4oz chopped nuts and seeds (toasted)
2 tbsp curried mayonnaise (mayonnaise with added curry powder - mix curry powder in a little water and add to mayonnaise)

Cut the vegetables into small pieces and place in boiling water for one minute. Drain and let go cold.
Mix with mayonnaise. Sprinkle with chopped nuts and seeds.

CURRY LENTIL SALAD

225g / 8oz lentils
250ml / $^{1}/_{2}$pt of stock or water
2 tomatoes chopped
2 scallions chopped
1 tbsp oil
1 tbsp lemon juice
Grated rind of a lemon
1 tsp curry powder

Place lentils in pot with stock/water, boil for 20 mins.
Do not overcook, or let go mushy. Cool.
Add rest of ingredients and serve immediately.

CRAB SALAD

175g / 6oz cooked crab meat with seasoning added
1/4 cucumber
2 tomatoes
110g / 4oz shredded lettuce
1 tbsp mayonnaise
1 tbsp natural bio yogurt
1 tbsp lemon juice

Mix the crab with the mayonnaise, lemon and yogurt. Serve on the shredded lettuce, tomato and cucumber. Garnish with lemon wedge.

TIP
Cabbage is good for the protection and treatment of stomach ulcers, cancer prevention, good for anaemia, respiratory disease and acne.

SPINACH AND BACON SALAD

4 rashers cooked till crispy
175g / 6oz baby spinach leaves
Chopped onion
1 tbsp walnut oil
1 tbsp olive oil
1 tbsp lemon juice
1 tbsp sesame seeds

Grill rashers till crispy. Cut into strips. Remove stalks from the spinach, place in a bowl, add onion, bacon and dressing just before serving. Sprinkle with toasted sesame seeds.

WALDORF SALAD

2 red apples / 2 green apples
2 sticks of celery
50g / 2oz of walnuts
2 tsp mayonnaise
2 tsp yogurt
2 tsp lemon juice

Cut apples into chunks. Mix with sliced celery and chopped walnuts. Combine with dressing (mayonnaise, yogurt, lemon juice).

COLESLAW

225g / 8oz shredded white and red cabbage
175g / 6oz carrots grated
1 stick celery grated
1 onion sliced / grated
1 red pepper chopped
2 tbsp mayonnaise / olive oil
Seasoning

Combine all ingredients, add seasoning and mix with mayonnaise.

PASTA OR RICE SALAD

225g / 8oz cooked rice or pasta with seasoning added
1 red pepper chopped
$1/2$ medium cucumber chopped
2 scallions chopped
1 onion sliced
1 carrot grated

Combine all ingredients together, mix well

TIP

To prevent high cholesterol eat dairy products in moderation only. Cut down on buns, biscuits, cakes and confectionery

POTATO SALAD

450g / 1lb potatoes
2 scallions
1 small onion chopped
1 tbsp mayonnaise
1 tbsp yogurt
2 rashers fried until crispy
Seasoning

Cut potatoes into cubes and boil. Do not overcook.
Let go cold, combine with bacon strips, onion, scallions and seasoning.
Mix in mayonnaise and yogurt.

TABOULI

225g / 8oz bulgar wheat / cous cous (soaked in 275ml / $1/2$ pt of boiling water)
4 scallions
4 tomatoes de-seeded and skin removed
2 dsp oil
1 dsp lemon juice
Cucumber chopped

Soak the bulgar wheat / cous cous in boiling water for 15–20 mins until all the water is absorbed. Let go cold.
Add all remaining ingredients.

TIP

Onions and garlic are good for the heart and circulation. They also contain natural antibiotics. Also good for candida sufferers.

VEGETABLES

POLENTA

225g / 8oz coarsely ground corn maize meal
450ml / ¾ pt water / home-made stock

Mix 2 tbsps of water with the corn.
Boil remainder of water / stock and gently pour in corn.
Stir while pouring.
Bring back to the boil and cover.
Simmer for 30 mins. Stir occasionally.

VARIATIONS:
Mix with chopped vegetables or nuts, pour onto an oiled greaseproof tray and bake or roll into a sausage shape.
Slice and fry.

RICE BALLS

Shape cooked brown rice into balls (wet hands in cold water to prevent sticking).
Roll in toasted sesame seeds or chopped nuts.

SOYA BEAN CURRY

175g / 6oz soya beans or any beans of choice
1 large onion chopped
1 large apple grated
2 cloves garlic crushed
2 tbsp oil
1 dsp curry powder
1 dsp plain flour / rice flour / potato flour
1 tsp lemon juice
1 tsp sugar (optional)
150ml / 1/4 pt water

Soak beans overnight and cook slowly for 2 hrs until soft. Sauté onion, garlic and curry powder. Add apple and flour. Mix well. Add lemon juice, sugar, soya beans and water. Simmer for 15–20 mins. Serve with rice / pasta / potato / salad.

LENTIL BOLOGNESE

110g / 4oz lentils – washed
1 onion chopped
1/2 green pepper chopped
75g / 3oz mushroom sliced
1 carrot diced
1 stick celery sliced
6 tomatoes chopped
1/2 tsp chilli powder
1/2 tsp curry powder
2 cloves of garlic
275ml 1/2 pt stock/water

Sauté the onion and garlic, add remaining vegetables and

seasoning. Then add stock/water.
Bring to the boil and simmer covered for 1/2 hr until lentils are soft. (Add any vegetable of choice). Serve with pasta or as a filling for baked potatoes.

NUT AND VEGETABLE LOAF

1 onion finely chopped

1 clove garlic

50g / 2oz mushrooms chopped

50g / 2oz peas

3 tomatoes diced

1 dsp oil

1 carrot grated

1 apple grated

110g / 4oz cooked brown rice

50g / 2oz finely ground nuts

1/2 tsp chilli pepper

1 egg beaten

Sauté onion and garlic until soft. Add mushroom, peas, carrot, apple and tomato, sauté for another 2 mins.
Add remaining ingredients and mix well.
Place mix in a greased loaf tin.
Bake in a pre-heated oven for 40 mins at Gas mark 6, 400° F, 200° C.
Serve hot or cold with salads.

TIP
Extra virgin olive oil contains essential fatty acids needed for a healthy heart, use it in its pure form in salad dressings, add to mashed potato, stews, casseroles or soups just before serving.

VEGGIE BURGERS

2 grated potatoes
1 grated carrot
1 grated onion (or any vegetable of your choice)
1 garlic clove crushed
50g / 2oz broccoli pieces chopped fine
50g / 2oz diced mushrooms
1 egg or part allowed
Little plain flour / rice flour / wheat flour / potato flour

Mix vegetables and egg together. Make into burger shapes with floured hands. Fry slowly until cooked through.
OPTIONAL: You may also use chopped nuts / seeds, cooked flaked fish or cooked minced chicken.

SPANISH OMELETTE

1-2 tsp oil
1 onion finely chopped
2 cloves garlic finely chopped
175g / 6oz cooked fish / natural ham or chicken finely chopped (optional)
1 small green pepper (de-seeded and diced)
4 eggs beaten with 1 tbsp of cold water / milk / soya milk
50g / 2oz cheese (optional)
2 tomatoes chopped
1 cooked potato diced
Seasoning

Heat the oil in a large pan, sauté onion and garlic for a few minutes, then add diced potato. Add the meat or fish (optional) and continue to cook for 2–3 mins, add pepper and tomatoes.

Season eggs and pour into pan on top of mixture, sprinkle grated cheese on top. Allow to cook on the bottom, then place under a pre-heated grill until golden brown.

TIP
Eat regular meals and it is important that you have the time to enjoy and digest your food.

CHEESE AND POTATO BAKE

8 medium sized potatoes (peeled)
1 ciove of garlic crushed
25g / 1oz butter / oil
110g / 4oz cheese grated
450ml / 3/4pt milk / soya milk
Seasoning

Slice potatoes very thinly. Slice and pat dry. Rub the inside of an oven-proof dish with oil / butter. Arrange potatoes in layers sprinkling a little of the grated cheese between the layers. Heat the milk in a saucepan, add seasoning, crushed garlic and pour over potato layers, sprinkle remaining cheese on top. Place into a pre-heated oven Gas mark 4, 350° F, 180° C for approx. 45 mins or until potatoes are cooked and liquid is absorbed. Serve hot.

TIP
Liver is high in iron and zinc, it also contains vitamin A and B complex.

TIP
A well balanced diet with a wide variety of food prevents the need for vitamin supplements.

RATATOUILLE

1 onion chopped
1 clove of garlic crushed
1 tbsp oil
1 aubergine diced
8 tomatoes finely chopped
½ green pepper chopped
½ red pepper chopped
1 stick celery chopped
Seasoning

Heat oil, fry garlic and onion, add remaining vegetables. Add seasoning. Bring to the boil and simmer for 35 mins until vegetables are tender.
Serve with pasta dishes.

CABBAGE WITH GARLIC

450g / 1lb red / white / green cabbage shredded
2 tbsp oil
½ onion finely chopped
1 clove garlic crushed
Seasoning

Heat oil in saucepan. Sauté garlic and onion until soft. Add the shredded cabbage, stir. Add seasoning and cook for 10 mins with the lid on.

TIP
Eat to live, not live to eat.

GARLIC MUSHROOMS

450g / 1lb mushrooms
3 cloves garlic crushed
175g / 6oz butter
1 tbsp lemon juice
Salt and pepper

Prepare mushrooms, combine the butter, crushed garlic, lemon juice, salt and pepper. Arrange mushrooms – skin side down in a dish. Place the butter mix into each one.
Bake in a pre-heated oven for 10–15 mins at Gas mark 7, 425° F, 220° C.

BAKED PARSNIPS

1lb / 450g parsnips
1oz / 25g butter / 1 tbsp oil
2 tsp sugar (optional)

Cut parsnips into lengths and blanch in boiling salted water for 3 mins. Then place in a pre-heated greased dish, coating each piece with butter / oil.
Sprinkle sugar on top.
Bake in a pre-heated oven for 40 mins at Gas mark 6, 400° F, 200° C until golden brown turning them over once during that time.

BAKED STUFFED TOMATOES

4 large tomatoes
1 tbs oil
1 onion chopped
4 mushrooms chopped
3 tbs cooked rice / breadcrumbs
50g / 2 oz grated cheese
2 garlic cloves crushed
seasoning

Cut a thin slice off the stalk end of the tomatoes, scoop out the centres leaving shells but retaining pulp. Heat oil, sauté onion and garlic, add mushrooms and seasoning, stir in rice / breadcrumbs and tomato pulp. Fill the tomato shells with the mixture. Replace tomato top. Place in a greased baking dish.
Bake for 20 minutes in a preheated oven at Gas mark 6, 350° F, 180° C.
OPTIONAL: Substitute red peppers for tomatoes

CARNIVAL SALAD

225g /8 oz cooked fish of choice (prawns)
75 g / 3 oz cooked pasta shells
50g / 2 oz cucumber sliced
2 hard boiled eggs chopped
2 tomatoes chopped
25g / 1 oz lettuce shredded

Chop fish into a bowl (add prawns whole), add other ingredients except the lettuce, carefully stirring together, divide the lettuce between four glasses and spoon fish mixture on top.

LUNCHES
DINNERS

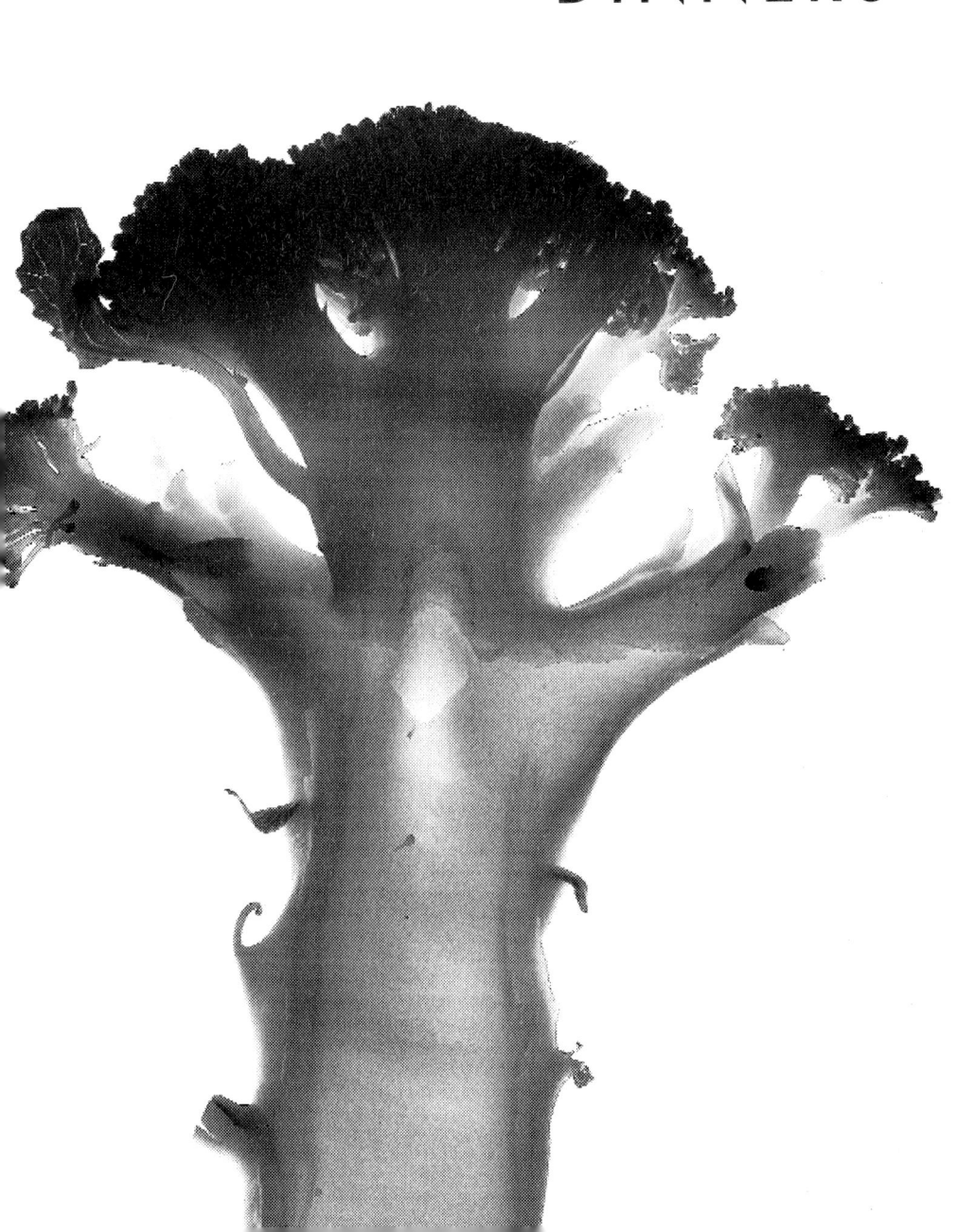

TIP
Avocado is excellent for the skin, helps in the relief of PMS, is good for the heart and circulation.

TIP
People with arthritis should avoid cooked potatoes however juice from raw may help the condition and also treat stomach ulcers.

LUNCH & DINNER IDEAS

- Home-made soups
- Baked potatoes – various fillings
- Salads
- Stir fries
- Stews
- Casseroles
- Fish / meat / steamed vegetables / potato
- Egg fried rice and vegetables
- Pasta dishes
- Open sandwiches – various fillings
- Potato cakes / veggie burgers
- Omelettes / scrambled eggs
- Mixed grill
- Fish dishes
- Vegetarian dishes
- Savoury pancakes
- Home-made burgers / fish and chips occasionally
- Cabbage and bacon

LUNCH & DINNERS

LENTIL AND TUNA BAKE

175g / 6oz red lentils
1 large onion finely chopped
1 dsp olive oil
1 large egg
150ml / ¼pt milk / soya milk
75g / 3oz tuna
Seasoning
2 tbsp chopped nuts and seeds

Bring lentils to the boil in a pint of water and simmer for 20–25 mins. Sauté onions, beat egg and milk together. Flake the tuna, combine all the ingredients except nuts and seeds and mix well. Pour mix into a greased ovenproof dish. Sprinkle nuts and seeds on top. Bake in a pre-heated oven at Gas mark 4, 350°F, 180°C for 30 mins approx.

RICE FISH CAKES

225g / 8oz cooked long grain rice
350g / 12oz fish (cod / haddock / salmon)
A little oil
1 onion chopped
Grated rind and juice of 1 lemon
2 egg yolks or 1 whole egg
1 grated potato
Seasoning

Poach fish – Remove skin, bones and flake.
Mix all ingredients together, shape with floured hands and fry.

TIP
Eggs are high in protein, a rich source of zinc, vitamins A, D, E, B and especially B12 (particularly good for vegetarians).

POTATO WEDGES

4 large potatoes
2 tsp chilli powder
A little oil
50g / 2oz of grated cheese (optional)

Wash potatoes well, cut in half lengthwise and then cut each half in half again like wedges. Coat wedges lightly in oil. Place on an ovenproof dish, skin side downwards. Sprinkle with chilli powder, cook in a pre-heated oven at Gas mark 6, 400°F, 200°C, for 50 mins.
Before the end of cooking time sprinkle grated cheese on top.

POTATO CAKES

275g / 10oz grated raw potato or cold mashed potato
1 onion
1 egg / 1 yolk / 1 white
50g / 2oz brown flour / rice flour / soya flour / potato flour
2 tsp oil

Mix potato, onions, egg and flour together. With floured hands, form into mini pancakes and fry in the oil until crisp and golden.

COLCANNON

1lb / 450g potatoes, peeled and quartered
2 onions finely chopped
$1/2$ white cabbage cored and finely sliced
2 parsnips
3 cabbage leaves
$1/2$ pt / 275ml water
Seasoning

Line the bottom of a deep saucepan with potato pieces on top of this place a layer of onions, then a layer of cabbage, then a layer of parsnips. Repeat until all ingredients are used up. Place seasoning in $1/2$ pt / 250ml of water and pour in. Top it off with the cabbage leaves. Cover with the lid and gently bring to the boil.
Simmer for 1 hr – remove the cabbage leaves from the top and mash all the cooked vegetables together.

TIP
Salt levels should not exceed $1/8$ oz daily – the level at which there is no risk of stomach cancer, high blood pressure or fluid retention and no loss of calcium in the bones. Start by taking the salt cellar off the table. Only use natural sea salt sparingly.

HOME-MADE OVEN CHIPS

Cut potatoes into thick chips and dry, pour oil into a dish and toss chips in it. Spread onto a baking tray and bake in a pre-heated oven for 40 mins at Gas mark 4, 350°F, 180°C – turning occasionally.

BAKED POTATOES

Wash the potatoes, scrub the skin and pat dry. Prick all over with a fork to allow steam to escape and prevent potatoes from bursting in the oven. Bake in a pre-heated oven at Gas mark 6, 400f°F, 200°C for 1½ hrs until tender.

When cooled, cut across the top of each baked potato or slice in half and top with desired filling.

FILLING IDEAS

- Salad mix – lettuce, onions, tomato, cucumber, red / green / yellow peppers, celery, sprouts, garlic and salad dressing
- Grated carrot, chopped pineapple and walnut
- Peppers, mushrooms, onions
- Tomato, onions, grated cheese
- Chilli con carne / bolognese
- Stir fry chicken / beef / fish / vegetable
- Celery, apple, chopped nuts and salad dressing
- Tuna and salad mix.
- Garlic butter
- Rasher, grated cheese and onion
- Top with sauces of choice, add vegetables, serve with salads

TIP
To guarantee adequate calcium intake, drink milk, eat a selection of the following each day – tofu, sesame seeds, natural bio yogurt, almonds, green leafy vegetables, lentils, watercress and apricots.

FAN BAKED POTATO

Using a sharp knife, slice the potatoes thinly at $^1/_4$ inch intervals without cutting all the way through to the end.
Place on a baking sheet and bake for 15 mins. Remove the baking sheet from the oven. Gently press down potatoes to fan and brush all over with the oil and season. Bake for a further 45 mins until tender and golden brown.

PANCAKES

1 large egg or 2 egg yolks	Batter (can
275ml / $^1/_2$ pt milk / soya milk	be used to coat fish,
110g / 4oz plain flour / soya flour / rye flour / wholemeal flour / rice flour / maize meal	meats or foods befor
Oil / butter	frying)

Mix the egg and milk together. Sift flour into egg mixture beating well until it thickens.
Heat oil in the pan until very hot, add mix cook one side, toss and cook other side until golden brown.

SWEET PANCAKE

Add sugar, top with mashed banana, strawberry, stewed fruit, home-made ice cream or fresh cream. Optional – add grated rind of an orange/lemon to batter mix.

SAVOURY PANCAKES

Top with flaked fish, salad, chicken, stir fry mix, back rashers, grated cheese or vegetables. Add a little chilli powder, black / white pepper, crushed garlic or sea salt to the batter mix.

PASTA AND TUNA

225g / 8oz wheat pasta / corn pasta / rice pasta
1 red pepper
25g / 1oz butter / oil
110g / 4oz mushrooms sliced
225g / 8oz peas
225g / 8oz can tuna in brine drained and flaked
110g / 4oz cheese
Seasoning

Cook pasta in boiling water according to instructions on pack. Drain. Melt oil, cook onion, garlic and mushrooms. Add red pepper, peas, tuna and pasta. Add cheese. Place over low heat until well heated through.
Add seasoning to taste and serve immediately.

HOME-MADE BURGERS

2 tsp plain flour / brown flour / rice flour / potato flour
450 g / 1lb lean minced beef / lamb / pork / chicken or turkey
2 potatoes peeled and grated
1 onion finely chopped
1 egg yolk (optional)
Seasoning

Mix all ingredients together. Form into round cakes with a floured hand and flatten. Grill or fry as desired. Give the burgers at least 5 mins on each side before you turn them. Cook until well done.

TIP
Lemon in boiling hot water is good for fighting infections of the respiratory tract.

CHILLI CON CARNE

1 onion chopped
1/2 green pepper chopped
2 sticks of celery chopped
1 clove garlic peeled and crushed
175g / 6oz carrot peeled and chopped
350g / 12oz lean minced beef
350g / 12oz tomato skinned and chopped
275ml / 1/2pt home-made stock / water
1 level tsp chilli powder
2 tsp natural curry powder
275g / 10oz soya beans / red kidney beans (cooked)
Little salt and pepper

Sauté minced beef, add onion, garlic and all seasonings. Cook for 10 mins. Add remaining ingredients, bring to the boil, cover and cook over gentle heat for 30–40 mins, stirring occasionally. To thicken, add a little flour and water, mixed together. Serve with long grain brown rice. Optional – sprinkle with grated cheese.

CHICKEN CASSEROLE

4 chicken breasts
3 large carrots chopped
1 clove of garlic crushed
2 onions chopped
50g / 2oz mushrooms sliced
275ml / 1/2pt home-made chicken stock / water
2 tsp lemon juice
Seasoning

Place chicken in a dish with carrots, onions, garlic and mushrooms. Pour in stock / water, lemon juice and seasoning. Bake in a pre-heated oven at Gas mark 4, 350°F, 180°C for 1 to 1½ hrs or until chicken is well cooked. Serve with baked potatoes.

FISH BAKE

450g / 1lb cod / haddock skinned and boned
275ml / ½pt milk / soya milk
1 onion peeled and chopped
1 clove garlic chopped
25g / 1oz plain flour / rice flour / potato flour
50g / 2oz mushrooms sliced
110g / 4oz baby corn
2 sticks celery finely diced
Seasoning

TOPPING:
450g / 1lb potatoes roughly diced and boiled for 2 to 3 mins
50g / 2oz cheese (optional)

Poach fish in milk with onion and garlic for 8 to 10 mins. Strain milk into saucepan, add seasoning, bring to the boil stirring constantly and cook for 2–3 mins. Add fish, mushrooms, celery, baby corn and mix carefully together. Place in ovenproof dish. Place potatoes on top of fish mixture and sprinkle with grated cheese.
Bake in a pre-heated oven at Gas mark 5, 375°F, 190°C for 15 to 20 mins until golden brown. Serve with salad.

TIP
If you take sport seriously remember that good nutrition is just as important as training.
Running for example needs a slow release complex carbohydrate – e.g. pasta or brown rice

KEDGEREE

350g / 12oz cod / haddock
175g / 6oz brown long grain rice cooked
110g / 4oz peas
1 clove garlic crushed
1 egg hard boiled and chopped
2 tbsp milk / soya milk
1 tsp freshly squeezed lemon
Seasoning
1 tsp of curry powder (optional)

Place fish in shallow pan of cold water. Add clove of crushed garlic. Bring slowly to the boil and simmer for 10 to 15 mins. Drain, flake and remove skin and bones. Mix with rice, peas, eggs, milk, lemon juice and seasoning. Place mixture in ovenproof dish. Cover and cook in pre-heated oven at
Gas mark 3, 325°F, 170°C for 15 to 20 mins.

TIP
One third of your food should consist of fruit, salad, vegetables. Eat five portions a day for their vitamins, minerals, fibre and protective phyto-chemicals.

SPAGHETTI BOLOGNESE

1 onion chopped
1/2 green pepper chopped
2 sticks of celery chopped
1 clove garlic crushed
175g / 6oz carrot chopped
350g / 12oz round steak / lamb / pork / minced
3 back rashers
350g / 12oz tomato skinned and chopped
275ml / 1/2 pt home-made stock / water
Seasoning

Heat a little oil, cook onion and garlic. Add meat and rashers, cook for a further 10 mins, then add all remaining ingredients. Bring to the boil. Cover and cook over gentle heat for 30 to 40 mins stirring occasionally and adding more water if required. Serve with cooked spaghetti, tagliatelle or macaroni.

SHEPHERDS PIE

Use spaghetti bolognese recipe and potato topping.

POTATO TOPPING:

450g / 1lb peeled and boiled potatoes
2 to 3 scallions
Seasoning
75g / 3oz grated cheese (optional)

Mash all ingredients together. Put the bolognese mixture into a greased baking dish. Spread the mashed potato on top.
Bake in a pre-heated oven for 30 mins at Gas mark 6, 400°F, 200°C until golden brown.
10 mins before end of cooking time sprinkle with grated cheese.

STUFFED ROAST TURKEY BREAST

2 turkey breast joints
225g / 8oz back rashers
A little oil
1 small onion chopped
1–2 cloves garlic crushed
225g / 8oz mushrooms sliced
Seasoning
1 tsp finely grated lemon rind

Fry the onion and garlic together in oil.
Add mushrooms and fry until they soften. Put in the food processor to chop finely, almost like breadcrumbs, and put into a bowl. Fry the rashers. Put into the food processor to chop finely. Add to the mushrooms and onions and the rest of the ingredients and mix together. Allow to cool.
The breast has a natural division like a pocket, cut with a sharp knife to make this pocket even bigger. Put the cold stuffing into the pocket. Sit the joints on a foil lined tin. Fold the foil completely over the turkey. Roast in the oven until cooked through.
Roast for about 45 mins in a pre-heated oven at Gas mark 6, 400°F, 200°C, then reduce to Gas mark 4, 350°F, 180°C, and cook for another 20–30 mins.
Turn back the foil for the last 15–20 mins of cooking.
Substitute turkey with chicken breast joints.

TIP
Small amounts of pure natural butter are far better for you than lots of chemical margarines which have the same amount of calories.

TIP
Melon is a good source of vitamin A. It is good for constipation, urinary problems, gout and arthritis.

LASAGNE

Make up spaghetti bolognese recipe (see page 65). (Substitute beef with minced pork, lamb or chicken if desired)

50g / 2oz plain flour / rice flour / potato flour
50g / 2oz butter
1 pt / 570 ml milk / soya milk
75g / 3oz / grated cheese (optional)
6–8 sheets plain lasagne (pasta)

To make white sauce see page 31.
Grease a shallow ovenproof dish and cover with a layer of bolognese mix. Add a layer of pasta and white sauce. Repeat the layers two or three times finishing with a layer of white sauce. Top with grated cheese. Bake in a pre-heated oven at Gas mark 6, 400°F, 200°C for 30 mins.
Serve with mixed salad.

TIP
Fish, eggs and sunlight provide vitamin D. These factors with gentle regular exercise help to provide strong bones and support muscles. Excess amounts of coffee, tea, alcohol and smoking can hinder calcium absorption.

LENTIL PIE

225g / 8oz red lentils
450g / 1lb tomatoes skinned and blended
1 onion
2 red peppers
225g / 8oz mushrooms
Selection of other vegetables
450g / 1lb potatoes boiled and mashed
275ml / $1/2$ pt of water

Place the oil in a large frying pan and fry vegetables, onions, mushrooms and peppers for 5 mins. Add lentils and tomatoes, add water, mix well.

Place mixture in a casserole dish. Top with mashed potatoes. Bake in a pre-heated oven for 20 mins at Gas Mark 6, 400°F, 200°C or until mashed potato is brown.

LAMB AND ORANGE HOTPOT

1 onion chopped
25g / 1oz butter / oil
2 cloves garlic crushed
450g / 1lb lean stewing lamb pieces
450g / 1lb carrots sliced
3 sticks celery chopped
150ml / $1/4$ pt natural orange juice (2 oranges)
720ml / $1 1/4$ pt home-made stock / water
Seasoning
1 tsp sugar
2 tsp plain flour / rice flour / potato flour

Sauté onion in butter / oil, add garlic. Next fry lamb pieces until browned. Transfer to a saucepan. Add all remaining ingredients except flour. Bring to the boil, simmer gently until meat is tender for approx. 1 hr. Blend the flour with a little water and add to the saucepan. Bring to the boil stirring to thicken.
Serve with boiled / baked or mashed potatoes.

CHICKEN BREASTS IN WHITE SAUCE

2 chicken breasts
1/4pt / 150ml milk / soya milk
1/4pt / 150ml of home-made chicken stock
4oz / 110g mushrooms sliced
1 garlic clove crushed
1/2 onion chopped finely
2 tsp plain flour / rice flour / potato flour
Seasoning

Place chicken breasts into saucepan with milk, stock and seasoning. Put in the mushrooms, onions and garlic. Bring to the boil and then simmer with the lid on until chicken is cooked – (approx. 15 mins).
Lift out chicken breasts and keep warm.
Blend flour with a little water and add to the saucepan.
Stir until mixture thickens. Pour over the chicken.
Serve with steamed vegetables and baked potato or rice.
OPTIONAL: Turkey breasts may be used instead of chicken.

TIP
Avoid processed foods and eat home-made soups, vegetables, casseroles, stews and natural foods.

TROUT WITH MUSHROOMS

2 trout fillets or fish of choice
A little oil
1 onion chopped
2 cloves garlic chopped
225g / 8oz mushrooms chopped
Seasoning
1 tbsp lemon juice
2 tbsp natural yogurt

Heat oil and fry the onion and garlic, add mushrooms, seasoning and lemon juice. Stir in natural yogurt. Place trout in ovenproof dish. Spoon mixture over same. Cover with foil. Bake in a pre-heated oven for 30 mins approx. at Gas mark 5, 375°F, 190°C.

BAKED MACKEREL WITH STUFFING

2 whole mackerel cleaned and gutted
Juice of 1/2 lemon
50g / 2oz wholemeal breadcrumbs
2 stalks of celery finely chopped
1 onion chopped
1 clove garlic chopped
50g / 2oz toasted almonds
Seasoning

Mix lemon juice, breadcrumbs, celery, onion and garlic. Add seasoning. Place stuffing inside fish. Put in an ovenproof dish and cover with foil. Bake in a pre-heated oven at Gas mark 5, 375°F, 190°C for 30–40 mins.
Remove foil for last 10 mins of cooking. Sprinkle with toasted almonds. Substitute mackerel with trout or herring.

BACON AND LIVER CASSEROLE

225g / 8oz liver
2 dsp seasoned plain flour / rice flour / potato flour
Little oil
6 back rashers
2 onions sliced
450ml / ¾ pt home-made stock
Seasoning

Coat liver with seasoned flour. Heat oil and fry rashers. Then place in a casserole dish. Fry onion and liver until lightly brown. Transfer to dish, pour in stock and cover. Cook until tender for 1½–2 hrs in a pre-heated oven at Gas mark 3, 325°F, 170°C. To thicken, add remaining flour and water mixed.
OPTIONAL: Cook layered with breadcrumbs on top.

FISHERMANS PIE

275g / 10oz white fish / cod / haddock or any fish of choice.
175g / 6oz prawns
450g / 1lb mashed potatoes
Seasoning

SAUCE:
25g / 1oz butter
25g / 1oz flour
275ml / ½ pt milk / soya milk
Seasoning

Cut fish into chunks, add seasoning. Make up white sauce.(See page 31). Place prawns and white fish in dish and cover with sauce. Top with a layer of potato. Bake in a pre-heated oven for 45 mins at Gas mark 3, 325°F, 170°C.

STEW

450g / 1lb lean stewing beef / pork pieces, mutton or gigot chops
6 carrots diced
2 parsnips diced
$1/2$ turnip diced
1 stick celery chopped
2 onions chopped
2 cloves garlic chopped
450g / 1lb potatoes cut in sections
2 dsp oil
1 dsp plain flour / rice flour / potato flour
Seasoning
570ml / 1pt home-made stock / water

Dip the meat pieces in seasoned flour. Heat oil in the bottom of a large pot. Toss in meat and brown slightly. Add onion, garlic and cook until soft. Add pint of stock or water, bring to the boil and simmer for 30 mins. Add all remaining vegetables and simmer for a further 40–50 mins. Stir occasionally.

OPTIONS:
Add peas, mushrooms, red, green and yellow peppers
Add chopped tomatoes
Add soya beans
Add lentils
Add 1–2 tsp curry powder

STIR FRIES

Stir fries are quick, easy, very nutritious and tasty. They can be varied so much to suit individual tastes. The combination of meats / fish and plenty of vegetables give wonderful natural flavours.

TIPS ON STIR FRYING

- Prepare all ingredients before you start to cook
- Cut meat as thinly as possible
- Heat the pan / wok before adding oil
- Heat the oil before adding food
- Stir fry meat, poultry and seafood over high heat in batches so food has space to brown and seal quickly
- Add vegetables and cook until crunchy
- Stand over the pan / wok stirring and moving ingredients while stir frying. Also shake the pan / wok occasionally
- Stir fry just before serving as it only takes minutes
- If drying out add a little water rather than too much oil

STIR FRYING IDEAS

MEATS / FISH – choose favourite meats or combinations and cook
- Pork / bacon / rasher pieces
- Beef strips
- Lamb pieces
- Chicken / turkey pieces
- Prawns / tuna / cod / trout / haddock pieces
- Soya tofu curd

VEGETABLES – add lots of vegetables for added minerals and vitamins

- Aubergine
- Green Beans
- Broccoli pieces, cauliflower pieces, carrots
- Red / white cabbage shredded
- Courgette
- Red / green chillies
- Celery / mixed sprouts
- Baby corn
- Mushrooms
- Garlic / onion
- Red / green / yellow peppers
- Little grated parsnip / turnip / potato
- Chopped tomatoes
- Cooked soya beans

OPTIONAL –

- Pineapple chunks
- Grated apple
- Chopped nuts and seeds
- Curry / chilli powder

To make stir fries more juicy add –

- Stock from meat bones and thicken with flours of choice
- Tomato sauce mix, chopped tomatoes (see sauce section)
- Pineapple juice from fresh pineapples soaked overnight in boiling water
- a little fresh cream

SERVE STIR FRIES WITH –

- Brown / white rice
- Rice noodles / rice pastas / corn pastas / potatoes
- Wheat pastas / wheat noodles

BOILED BROWN RICE

2 cups brown rice

4 cups water

Wash and drain the rice. Bring water to the boil, add rice. Turn heat down, cover and simmer for 40 minutes until tender and water is absorbed. Do not stir while cooking as this breaks up the grains. Fluff with a fork when ready.

EGG FRIED RICE

225g / 8oz cooked rice

1 egg / 2 yolks

A little onion / garlic

A little grated carrot

Seasoning

Little oil

Heat pan / wok. Add oil, sauté onion / garlic. Add cooked rice, grated carrot and seasoning until heated through. Add beaten egg / yolks and mix well. Serve hot.

BUCKWHEAT / MILLET (RICE SUBSTITUTE)

Put grain in 4 times its volume of water, bring to the boil and simmer until soft and the water is absorbed, approx. 15 mins. Do not stir while cooking.

TIP
Have a mixed diet of as many different foods as possible. It gives the body extra nutrients.

THAI STYLE CHICKEN CURRY

2 chicken breasts chopped
1 onion finely chopped
3 garlic crushed
1 red chilli deseeded and finely chopped
1 tsp curry powder
570ml/ 1pt natural coconut milk
50g / 2oz coconut grated
110g / 4oz green beans
3 cabbage leaves shredded
Seasoning
A little oil

Heat oil, fry the chicken pieces until lightly brown. Add the garlic, onion, chilli, curry powder and seasoning. Stir and cook for 5 minutes. Add the coconut milk, stir well, bring to the boil and simmer for 10 minutes. Add the red pepper, green beans and cabbage. Fold in the grated coconut, cook for a further 10–15 minutes. Serve with rice.

TIP
Diabetics should eat a high fibre diet, especially wholegrain breads, pastas, lentils, rice, potatoes, porridge, fruit and vegetables.

BREADS
BAKING

Physical well-being is not only a priceless asset to oneself – it is a heritage to be passed on

BAKING TIPS
Don't quit, practice makes perfect!

- Pre-heat oven and cook at correct temperature
- Pre-heat baking trays / tins before greasing
- Add a little fresh lemon / grapefruit juice to milk to help raise bread
- Sift flours to add air
- Separate eggs and beat whites until fluffy, fold in at the end of bread making to help raise breads
- Add nuts, seeds, grated apple, grated carrot or mashed banana to breads for added nutrients and flavour
- Use bread soda (bicarbonate of soda) or gluten free baking powders as raising agents
- For gluten free breads you can use rice flour / rice bran / rice flakes / soya flour / soya bran / soya flakes or corn maize meal

Spreads and topping ideas for breads
- Butter
- Home-made jams, curds
- Mashed banana
- Strawberries / raspberries mashed with banana
- Stewed fruits (apple or rhubarb)
- Grated cheese

- Pure oils drizzled on top and heated under the grill
- Nut spreads (nuts, seeds and oil blended together)
- Mashed cooked egg
- Tomato
- Meats / fish / salad
- Fried bread
- French toast / plain toast
- Bread substitutes – natural rice / corn / or oat cakes

BREADS

TRADITIONAL BROWN BREAD

110g / 4oz plain white flour
225g / 8oz wholewheat flour
50g / 2oz wheatgerm
50g / 2oz wheatbran
1 egg / yolk / white
3 dsps oil
275ml or ½ pt milk / soya milk / juice / water
1 tsp bread soda / baking powder

Mix all dry ingredients. Mix wet ingredients.
Combine both until the mixture is able to drop off the spoon.
Pour into an oiled 900g / 2lb loaf tin.
Bake in a pre-heated oven for 50–60 mins at Gas mark 6, 400°F, 200°C.

HIGH FIBRE BROWN

275g / 10oz wholewheat flour
50g / 2oz wheatbran / wheatgerm
110g / 4oz pinhead oatmeal / oatbran / oatflakes
50g / 2oz chopped nuts and seeds
275ml / 1/2pt milk / soya milk / juice / water
2 tbsp oil
1 egg yolk / yolk / white
1 tsp bread soda / baking powder

Mix all dry ingredients. Mix wet ingredients. Combine both. Pour into a greased 900g / 2lb loaf tin. Bake in a pre-heated oven for 50–60 mins at Gas mark 6, 400°F, 200°C.
To make scones, make mixture less moist, mix to form a dough which sticks together. Roll out onto a floured board, cut into thick pieces, brush with egg, sprinkle with nuts and seeds.

WHOLEMEAL PASTRY

110g / 4oz plain white flour
110g / 4oz wholemeal flour
150ml or 1/4pt olive oil or 100g / 4oz butter
3–4 tbsp cold water
1 egg yolk

Mix dry ingredients, add butter / oil to dry ingredients and mix to resemble bread-crumbs, add egg and water to make dough mixture. Roll out and bake in a pre-heated oven at Gas mark 4, 350°F, 180°C for approx 30 mins or until golden brown.

Use for home-made quiches, savoury pies, pizza bases or apple / rhubarb tarts.

SWEET SCONES

225g / 8oz plain white flour
75g / 3oz granulated sugar
75g / 3oz butter
1 egg
¼pt / 150ml milk / soya milk
1 tsp bread soda / baking powder

FILLING:
Fresh strawberries 225g / 8oz
Juice of 1 orange
2 tsp sugar
¼pt / 150ml cream

Sieve the flour, soda / baking powder and sugar into a bowl. Add butter and rub into the flour until it resembles bread crumbs. Mix the egg and milk together – add to the dry ingredients to make a softish dough.
Spread lightly on a floured surface. Cut into thick pieces. Bake in a pre-heated oven until golden brown and cooked through, for 20–25 mins at Gas mark 5, 375°F, 190°C.
FILLING:- Mix strawberries, orange and sugar together. Chill. Serve with hot scones and whipped cream.

For **savoury scones** omit sugar, add grated onion, garlic, cheese, black and white pepper. Brush with milk and sprinkle with sesame seeds.

TIP
Lentils are high in fibre so they protect the body against bowel cancer. They also have plenty of B vitamins especially niacin which helps to lower stress and mental exhaustion.

CARROT CAKE

110g / 4oz butter or ¼pt / 150ml oil

110g / 4oz brown sugar

4 eggs beaten

225g / 8oz grated carrots

225g / 8oz plain flour / brown flour / rice flour

1 tsp bread soda / baking powder

50g / 2oz chopped nuts

1 tsp grated lemon zest

Heat the sugar and butter / oil together over a low heat until sugar is dissolved. Allow to cool slightly. Put egg and grated carrot into a bowl, add melted mixture. Sift in the flour and baking powder. Add nuts and lemon. Mix well to combine all ingredients. Transfer to a preheated, greased 20cm / 8in tin and bake for 1¼hr–1½hr at Gas mark 4, 350°F, 180°C until golden brown and well risen.

BARLEY BREAD

350g / 12oz barley flour

50g / 2oz soya bran

50g / 2oz chopped mixed nuts

425ml / ¾pt milk / soya milk

2 tbsp oil

1 egg / yolk / white

1 tsp baking powder / bread soda

½ grated apple / carrot

Place all ingredients in a food processor and mix well, or mix dry ingredients and wet ingredients separately. Combine both, add nuts, apple / carrot. Place in a greased 900g / 2lb loaf tin in a preheated oven for 45 mins approx at Gas mark 6, 400°F, 200°C.

CORN BREAD

400g / 14oz fine maize meal
50g / 2oz grated apple / carrot
1 tbsp oil
1 egg / yolk / white
275ml / 1/2pt milk / soya milk / water
1 tsp bread soda / baking powder
75g / 3oz chopped nuts

Place all ingredients together in a food processor or mix wet ingredients and dry ingredients separately. Combine both, add grated apple / carrot / nuts. Place in a 900g / 2lb greased loaf tin in a pre-heated oven for 45 mins approx at Gas mark 6, 400°F, 200°C

TIP

Tomatoes are low in salt, high in beta carotene, vitamin C and E, so help in the prevention of heart disease.

MIXED GRAIN BREAD

225g / 8oz oatmeal, oatbran mixed
75g / 3oz rye flour
150g / 5oz barley flour
2 tsp bread soda / baking powder
1 egg or 2 yolks
2 tbsp oil
275ml or 1/2pt milk / soya milk / juice

Mix dry ingredients. Mix wet ingredients. Combine both. Place in a 900g / 2lb loaf tin in a pre-heated oven for approx. 1 hr at Gas mark 4, 350°F, 190°C .

SPECIAL SOYA / RICE SCONES

| 110g / 4oz soya bran / rice bran |
| 350g / 12oz rice flour |
| 75g/ 3oz nuts and seeds chopped |
| 1 grated apple |
| 3 mashed bananas |
| ½ grated carrot |
| 1 egg / 2 yolks |
| 2 tbsp oil |
| 275ml or ½pt milk / soya milk |
| 1 tsp bread soda / baking powder |

Mix all dry ingredients, mix all wet ingredients – combine both until dough-like, roll, cut into thick pieces, brush with milk and sprinkle with seeds.
Bake in a pre-heated oven for 30–40 mins approx at Gas mark 6, 400°F, 200°C.

SHORTBREAD

| 175g / 6oz plain flour / rice flour |
| 50g / 2 oz sugar |
| 110g / 4oz butter |
| 1 tbsp milk / soya milk |

Grease and flour an 18cm / 7in circular tin.
Sift the rice flour and then add the sugar.
Rub in the butter and stir in the milk. Mix lightly to form a dough and press into the tin to a thickness of about 1¼cm or ½in. Prick the surface with a fork. Bake for 45 mins in a pre-heated oven at Gas mark 3, 325°F, 160°C.

TIP

Oily fish are beneficial for osteoarthritis, rheumatism, rheumatoid arthritis, eczema, psoriasis, most inflammatory diseases and heart protection.

RICE BREAD

350g / 12oz brown rice flour
110g / 4oz brown rice flakes / rice bran
1 egg / yolk / white
2 tbs oil
275ml / ½pt milk / soya milk
1 tsp bread soda / baking powder
Grated apple / carrot
Chopped nuts

Place all ingredients together in a food processor or mix all dry ingredients. Mix wet ingredients. Combine both until you have a soft dough. Add in grated carrot, apple and nuts, pour into a greased 900g / 2lb loaf tin.
Bake for 20 mins approx in a pre-heated oven at Gas mark 5, 375°F, 190°C.
Cover with foil and continue for 40 mins at Gas mark 3, 325°F, 170°C.

RYE BREAD SCONES

225g / 8oz rye flour, rye flakes mixed
275ml or ½pt milk / soya milk / fruit juice
2 tbsp chopped almonds
1 tsp bread soda

OPTIONAL:
Mashed banana, grated apple / carrot, nuts and seeds.
Mix all dry ingredients, add enough milk to make a light dry dough, roll, brush with milk, sprinkle with seeds or nuts and cut into thick pieces. Bake in a pre-heated oven for 40 mins at Gas mark 5, 375°F, 190°C.

APPLE AND WALNUT TEABREAD

| 225g / 8oz plain flour / rice flour |
| 110g / 4oz butter / 2 tbsp oil |
| 110g / 4oz brown sugar |
| 2 eggs |
| 110g / 4oz chopped walnuts |
| 1 tsp bread soda / baking powder |
| 1 apple grated |

Pre-heat oven to Gas mark 2, 300°F, 150°C.
Grease a 900g / 2lb loaf tin and line the base with grease proof paper.
Sift flour and baking powder / bread soda. Cream butter and sugar together. Beat in 1 egg and 1 tbsp rice flour.
Beat in second egg and stir in the remainder of the flour, nuts and apple.
Put mixture in tin and level it. Bake for 1–1½ hrs.
Turn out when cool.

TIP
Soya beans help in the prevention of hormone linked cancers – prostate, breast, ovarian and cervical. Can be eaten as tofu, soya milk, soya flour, soya bran and soya beans.

TIP

Live yogurt on a daily basis helps to relieve symptoms of thrush and cystitis.

Lettuce, particularly red lettuce, is very good during early stages of pregnancy or pre-conception as it contains folic acid, beta-carotene, vitamin C, some calcium and iron.

If prone to constipation eat fibre rich foods such as fruit, vegetables, nuts and seeds. Drink plenty of water and cut down on tea and coffee.

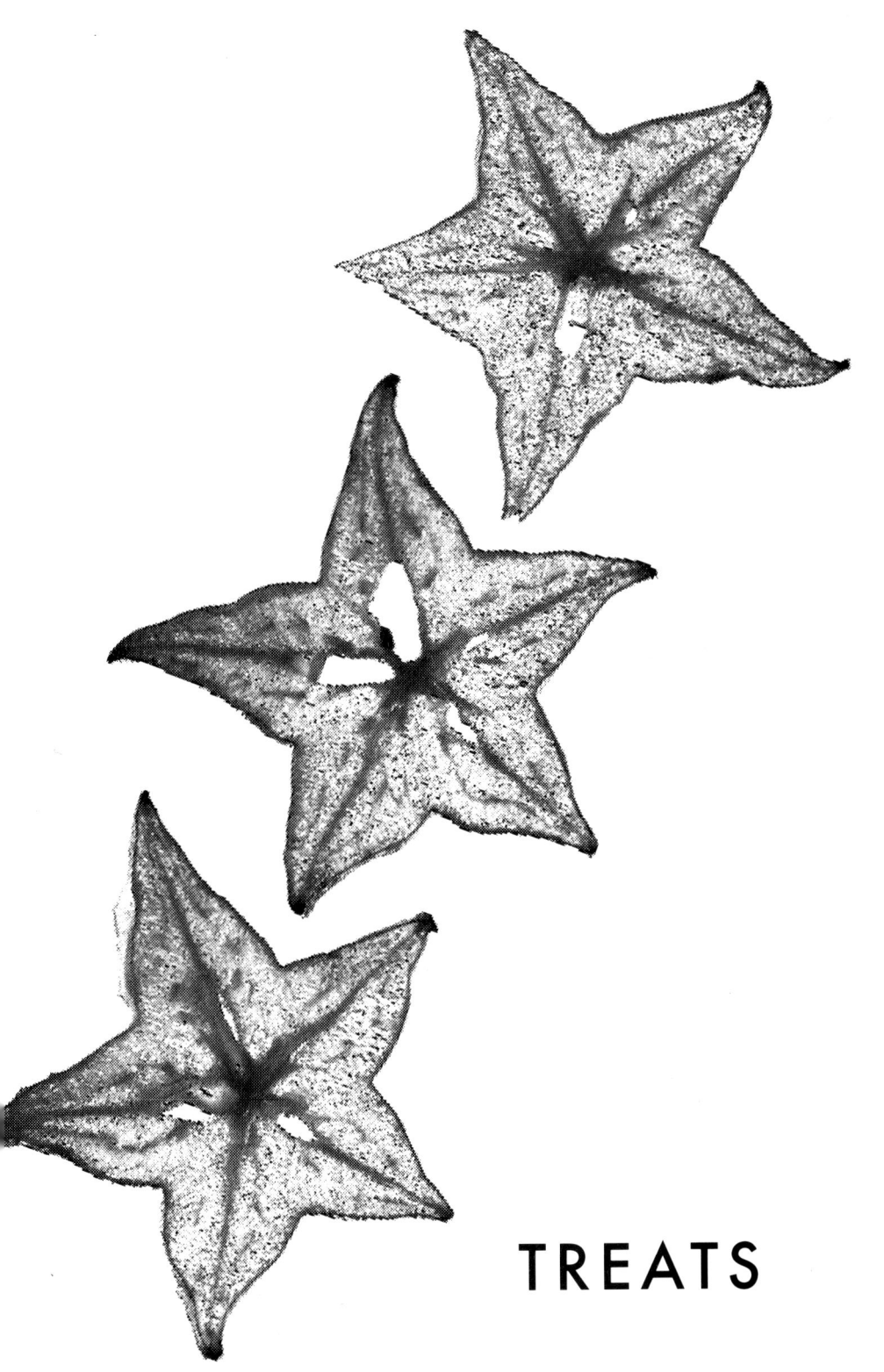

TREATS

HEALTH PROMOTING TIPS

- Eat well.
- Exercise most days.
- Get a good nights sleep.
- Have a laugh every day.
- Learn to relax.
- Say kind words daily.
- Drive carefully.
- Look after the environment.

TREATS

BANANAS OR PEACH IN ORANGE

4 bananas / peaches peeled and cut into thick slices
Grated rind and juice of 2 oranges
25g / 1oz toasted almonds
Natural yogurt

Place fruit in ovenproof dish. Pour orange juice with rind over fruit. Cover and bake in pre-heated oven Gas mark 4, 350°F, 180°C for 15 mins until fruit is just tender.
Serve hot, sprinkled with toasted almonds and yogurt.

NUTTY CRUMBLE

700g / 1½lb fruit (apples, rhubarb, oranges, strawberries)
50g / 2oz wholewheat flour
50g / 2oz porridge oats
50g / 2oz natural butter / 1 tbsp oil
50g / 2oz brown sugar
25g / 1oz walnuts or unsalted peanuts chopped

Prepare fruit, add sugar and nuts, place in an ovenproof dish. Mix together the flour with the oats and rub in butter / oil, until like breadcrumbs. Spoon over the fruit mixture.
Bake in pre-heated oven for 30 mins at Gas mark 4, 350°F, 180°C. Serve with natural bio yogurt or home-made custard. (See page 93).

POACHED PEARS WITH RASPBERRY / STRAWBERRY COULIS

275ml / ½ pt water

50g / 2oz sugar

4 pears

110g / 4oz strawberries / raspberries

50g / 2oz chopped almonds

Peel pears leaving stalks attached.
Poach in water and sugar for 20–25 mins covered.
Serve with puréed strawberries or raspberries.
Sprinkle with toasted almonds.

TIP

Peaches are salt and fat free, this makes them suitable for those with cholesterol and blood pressure problems.

STRAWBERRY AND MELON

225g / 8oz strawberries

½ melon (remove pips and outer skin)

Juice of 1 orange

Slice strawberries and cut melon into chunks.
Put them into a bowl with the orange juice. Chill and serve.
Also makes a nice starter.

TIP

To ensure optimum brain function feed your body with the following foods daily. Seeds, nuts, apples, beetroot, celery, carrots, oats, barley, wheatgerm and fish.

CUSTARD

2–3 large egg yolks
1 tsp sugar
275ml / $^{1}/_{2}$pt milk / soya milk

Put the egg yolks into a bowl with the sugar and mix well. Heat the milk in a saucepan but do not boil. Return egg mixture to the saucepan over a gentle heat stirring continuously until custard thickens. Add to stewed fruit, home-made crumble or tart.

NUTTY OAT BARS

110g / 4oz butter
110g / 4oz brown sugar
1 egg yolk
50g / 2oz flour
50g / 2oz oat flakes
Chopped walnuts / almonds

Beat butter, sugar and egg yolk until soft. Add flour, oat flakes and chopped nuts. Press mixture into a greased swiss roll tin and bake in a pre-heated oven for 15–20 mins at Gas mark 5, 375°F, 190°C. Cut into bars while warm but leave in tin until cold.

RICE PUDDING

75g / 3oz rice
570ml / 1pt milk / soya milk or water and milk mixed
25g / 1oz sugar

Boil rice and milk together, add sugar then simmer for 20 mins. Serve with stewed fruits, home-made jam or cream.

MERINGUES

110g / 4oz sugar
2 egg whites
Pinch of salt

Whisk egg whites, salt and sugar together over a pot of simmering water until stiff. Pipe mixture on to a greased baking tray. Bake in a pre-heated oven for $2^1/_2$–3 hrs at Gas mark $^1/_4$, 225°F, 110°C, alternatively use 2 dessert spoons dipped in cold water to shape oval meringues. Serve with fresh fruit salad, crushed strawberries or cream.

BANANA ICE-CREAM

450ml / ³/4pt milk
175g / 6oz sugar
3 eggs beaten
450ml / ³/4pt cream
6 mashed bananas

Put the milk, sugar and eggs in a saucepan and heat gently, stirring all the time until mixture thickens. Strain into a bowl – leave to cool. Whip the cream until slightly thickened and add to the cooled mixture. Stir in the mashed bananas.
Pour into a freeze-proof container, cover and freeze until firm. Place in the fridge 1 hr before serving to soften.
Substitute bananas with strawberries, pineapple or other fruits.
Do not refreeze home-made ice-creams.

TIP
Strawberries have a cleansing and purifying action, they are a great help for joint pains.

RHUBARB / APPLE SPONGE

450g / 1lb rhubarb / apple

75g / 3oz sugar

Juice and rind of 1 orange

75g / 3oz plain flour / rice flour

50g / 2oz wholewheat flour

110g / 4oz butter

110g / 4oz sugar

2 eggs

1 level tsp bread soda / baking powder

Prepare rhubarb, cut into pieces and put into an ovenproof dish. Add sugar, orange juice and rind on top of the rhubarb. Mix the flour and bread soda together. Beat the sugar and butter until fluffy, then beat in the eggs one at a time, adding some of the flour with each one. Add the remaining flour and mix in. Put mixture on top of rhubarb. Place in a pre-heated oven and cook until baked through for 45 mins. at Gas mark 5, 375°F, 190°c.

FRESH FRUIT SALADS

450g / 1lb natural fresh fruits of choice –

Apple, grapes, orange, pear, pineapple, melon, strawberries, peach, banana etc

275ml / 1/2pt fruit juice of choice

Cut the fruit into chunks. Add fruit juice.
Chill and serve with fresh cream or natural yogurt.

TIP

Apples are suitable for people who are suffering from arthritis, gout, colitis, diarrhoea, and gastro-enteritis.

STRAWBERRY OR RASPBERRY WATER ICE

275ml / ½pt water
75g / 3oz brown / white sugar
225g / 8oz strawberries / raspberries
1 tsp lemon juice
2 egg whites

Heat water and sugar together until sugar has dissolved. Bring to the boil and simmer gently for 10 mins. Simmer strawberries or raspberries gently in a little water for 10 mins until tender. Strain and make up purée to 275ml / ½ pt with water. Cool, add lemon juice and sugar syrup and pour into ice-tray. Freeze for about an hour until nearly firm. Whisk egg whites until stiff. Turn half frozen mixture into chilled bowl, whisk until smooth. Fold in egg whites, return mixture to ice-tray and freeze until firm.
Take out of freezer 5 mins before serving.

STRAWBERRY JAM

1kg / 2lbs 4oz strawberries
1kg / 2lbs 4oz natural sugar heated
Juice of 2 lemons – strained

Put the fruit, sugar and strained lemon juice into a greased saucepan. Heat slowly until sugar is dissolved, then boil steadily for 15 mins stirring frequently. Skim off scum from the surface of the jam. Pour into sterilised glass jars, seal with waxed paper discs and cover with tightly fitting cellophane tops. Keep in the fridge. Substitute strawberries for oranges, pineapple, pears, apples, rhubarb or mix fruits together for desired flavours.

FRESH LEMON/ORANGE CURD

Juice and rind of 1 lemon / orange

75g / 3oz sugar

2 eggs

50g / 2oz butter cut into pieces

Put the grated lemon/ orange rind into a bowl. Mix the juice and eggs together, pour over the sugar and add the butter. Place the bowl over a pan of simmering water. Stir frequently till thickened for approximately 20 minutes. Store in a clean dry jar with a screw top lid. Eat within one week.

CRISPY POPCORN BUNS

50g / 2oz popcorn

225g / 8oz dark organic chocolate

A little oil

Coat the bottom of the saucepan with a little oil, cover with a single layer of popcorn. Put the lid on and cook over a gentle heat until the corn pops. Shake well. Melt the chocolate, add the corn and spoon into bun cases. Allow to cool and set.

OPTIONAL – add chopped nuts, seeds and dried natural fruit.

OTHER TREATS

- Home-made popcorn
- Nuts and seeds / natural dried fruits
- Sweet pancakes
- Coffee with cream / coffee made with boiled milk
- Hot chocolate – chopped organic dark chocolate with boiled milk
- Ice pops from home-made fruit juices
- Home-made sweet scones
- Home-made jams
- Home-made chips / wedges
- Milk shakes

TIP

One glass of mixed carrot and celery juice each day makes a good diuretic remedy and relieves fluid retention.